France

NORTH
AMERICA

EUROPE

ASIA

AFRICA

SOUTH
AMERICA

AUSTRALIA

Clare Boast

Heinemann
LIBRARY

First published in Great Britain by Heinemann Library
Halley Court, Jordan Hill, Oxford OX2 8EJ
a division of Reed Educational and Professional Publishing Ltd

OXFORD FLORENCE PRAGUE MADRID ATHENS
MELBOURNE AUCKLAND KUALA LUMPUR SINGAPORE TOKYO
IBADAN NAIROBI KAMPALA JOHANNESBURG GABORONE
PORTSMOUTH NH CHICAGO MEXICO CITY SAO PAULO

Designed by AMR
Illustrations by Art Construction
Printed and bound in Malaysia by Times Offset (M) Sdn. Bhd.

01 00 99 98 97
10 9 8 7 6 5 4 3 2 1

ISBN 0 431 04540 2

British Library Cataloguing in Publication Data

Boast, Clare
Step into France
1. France – Geography – Juvenile literature
I. Title II. France
914.4

Acknowledgements
The Publishers would like to thank the following for permission to reproduce photographs:
ALLSPORT P. Rondeau p.26; Bridgeman Art Library/Giraudon p.29; Colorific! D. Berretty p.18, Boccon-Gibod/Black Star p.23, Carl Purcell p.7; J. Allen Cash Ltd pp.8, 24; Trevor Clifford pp.4, 12-13, 16-17, 19, 21, 25, 26; Robert Harding Picture Library Vandermarst p.14; Trip A. M. Bazalik p.6, C. Bland p.22, D. Brooker p.5, B. Hills p.9, W. Newlands p.20, D. Ray p.28, D. Saunders p.27, A. Tovy pp.10-11; ZEFA p.15.

Cover photograph reproduced with permission of:
  background: Tony Stone Worldwide, Michael Brusselle
  child: The Image Bank, Marc Grimberg.

Our thanks to Betty Root for her comments in the preparation of this book.

Every effort has been made to contact copyright holders of any material reproduced in this book. Any omissions will be rectified in subsequent printings if notice is given to the Publisher.

CONTENTS

INTRODUCTION

WHERE IS FRANCE?

France is in the west of Europe. France has borders with six other European countries.

France has coastlines on the Atlantic Ocean, the Mediterranean Sea and the English Channel. France is joined to the UK by a tunnel under the English Channel.

The capital city of France is Paris. Over 9 million people live there. The River Seine flows through the middle of the city.

The Eiffel Tower, built in 1889, is 300 m high. This is higher than many modern skyscrapers.

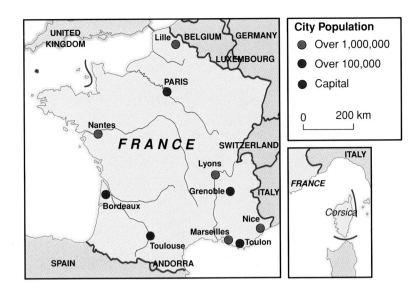

FRANCE'S HISTORY

France was part of the **Roman Empire** for about 500 years. Then it became lots of different countries. Part of it was ruled by England. France then became one country, ruled by one king. In 1789 there was a **revolution**. Kings were replaced by a **government** chosen by the people.

There are lots of places around the world where the local language is French. This is because France once owned land in Africa, America and other parts of the world.

The owners of this French castle make their living by selling wine from the grapes they grow.

5

THE LAND

It took the River Ardeche hundreds of years to make this gorge in the Massif Central.

PLATEAU

The Massif Central, in the middle and the south of France, is a **plateau**. The plateau is not all flat. There are old **volcanoes**, with lakes in the middle. There are puys – steep hills of **lava** from old volcanoes, worn by the weather.

Rivers have also worn away deep **gorges**, like the one in the picture on the left.

MOUNTAINS

France is separated from Spain by the Pyrenees mountains in the south. The Alps, in the south-east, separate France from Italy and Switzerland.

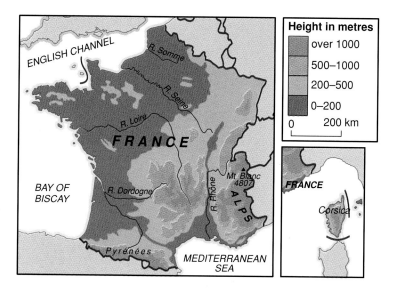

LOWLAND FRANCE

Most people in France live in the low, flattish land in the north and south-west of the country. Flat land is better for farming. It is also easier to build roads and buildings on flat land. There are some low hills and valleys made by rivers there, too.

Canals link many rivers. Rivers and canals are used to move things from place to place and for holiday boats.

This canal has been dug in the north of France, which is fairly flat.

WEATHER, PLANTS AND ANIMALS

Summer in the south of France. People work, shop and play games like boules (in the picture) in the cooler mornings or evenings.

THE WEATHER

Different parts of France have very different weather. The south has hot, dry summers and cool, wet winters. The north and west are cooler all year round.

It can be very cold in the east of France in winter. When the wind blows from the east, it brings cold air from the frozen parts of Russia. The mountains are coldest of all, with heavy snow in winter.

PLANTS AND ANIMALS

There are not many places in France where the land has not been cleared for homes or farming. Even much of the **scrubland** in the south has been cleared.

The mountains and the wet **marshlands** still have their natural plants, although some areas of marshland have been drained to use for farming.

There are not many wild animals left in France. There are some wolves and wild boar in the mountains.

The south of France has bad weather, too. It has storms in summer and a strong wind called the Mistral can blow at up to 100 kilometres per hour.

The Carmargue marshland in the south of France. Many animals and birds live wild here – there are not many people.

TOWNS AND CITIES

OLD TOWNS

Many of the towns and cities in France are very old. Some of them were first built in the time of the **Roman Empire**.

PARIS

Paris is an old city. The old part is the city centre, which has museums, art galleries and old churches as well as lots of shops and restaurants. This is the part of Paris that **tourists** visit.

A view of Paris and the River Seine. The centre of Paris is a mixture of old and new buildings.

Sometimes the family play Scrabble in the evening.

MEAL TIMES

The family have coffee, bread and jam for breakfast. They have lunch at work or school. They eat their main meal in the evening. They like to eat meat cooked in sauces and vegetables.

Camille and Leonard are practising their music together.

TIME OFF

The family live on one of the big shopping streets in the city. There is a lot to see and do close to home. They can go to shops, restaurants, cafés and parks.

The family like to spend time together at home, too. They play board games and the children play music. Tanguy also likes to go running to keep fit.

Tanguy rides his motorbike to work.

FARMING IN FRANCE

French farmers grow all sorts of different crops, depending on the weather, the soil and how high the land is.

GROWING WHEAT

Wheat grows best in the large, flat fields where it is easy to use ploughs and harvesting machines. Wheat needs soil that is not too dry. It needs rain to grow and sun to ripen.

KEEPING COWS

Cows are kept on dairy farms for their milk. A lot of the milk is made into butter and cheese. French butter and cheeses are famous all over the world.

Cows are kept in cool, wet areas where the grass grows well. Cows and sheep are also kept in places where it is too hilly to use farm machines.

OTHER CROPS

The south of France is hot and dry. It is a good place to grow sweetcorn and sunflowers, which are used to make cooking oil.

MAKING WINE

Grapes are grown in vineyards all over France, but mostly in the warm, dry south. The grapes are used to make wine. French wine is famous, and each area of France makes its own sort of wine. Each wine looks, smells and tastes different.

The grapes these people are picking will be made into wine.

People who know a lot about French wine know where it comes from by tasting and sniffing it. Sometimes they can even tell the name of the vineyard it came from!

LIVING IN THE COUNTRY

THE JUSSIAUX FAMILY

Dominique and Isabelle Jussiaux live in the country near Falaise. They have one girl, Camille (who is seven) and one boy, Thomas (who is four).

Isabelle and Dominique run a riding school, where children learn to ride horses. Isabelle is in charge of teaching riding. Dominique breeds and trains the horses so that they are safe to ride. The family have 40 horses in their stables. Isabelle and Camille both enter riding competitions in their spare time.

The family's house has a big garden and lots of land for the horses.

The family are eating pasta, rabbit stew and cheese for their evening meal.

THE FAMILY'S DAY

While Isabelle and Dominique are working, Camille goes to primary school and Thomas goes to nursery school. Isabelle drives them to school in Falaise, where she also shops for food.

MEALTIMES

The family eat bread with jam for breakfast. The children eat lunch at school but the family eat together in the evening.

The horses are kept in stables like these.

FRENCH SHOPS

SMALL SHOPS

France has lots of small shops that sell just one thing, like cheese or cakes. Very small shops in villages often sell a bit of everything, but most villages have a separate bakery.

BIG SHOPS

There are also big supermarkets that sell everything. The biggest ones, hypermarkets, are built on the edges of towns with lots of room for parking.

A hypermarket in France. They sell all sorts of things at lower prices than small shops.

Buying cheese from a market stall. Lots of the cheese is made by local farmers.

MARKETS

Some people still buy things from local markets, not supermarkets. Fruit and vegetables in the market are often fresher because they have come straight from local farms.

OPENING HOURS

Small local shops open at about 9 am and close for lunch. They then stay open into the late afternoon. They often have a day in the week when they are closed. Hypermarkets are open very early and late into the evening, to get as many customers as possible.

Now the Channel Tunnel is open, lots of English people go to France regularly to shop at the hypermarkets.

FRENCH FOOD

EATING OUT AND EATING IN

When French people go out to a big restaurant they often eat large meals that take a long time to make. But there are also places that sell cheap, fast food.

When people eat at home they often cook the main course, but get some food from special shops. They might have cold cooked meats to start the meal and tart or cake from the bakery to finish it.

Eating out in a restaurant. People often eat out with friends and spend all evening eating a meal.

Most French butchers cut, roll and stuff meat for their customers.

BREAD

People eat bread with almost every meal. Bakers make lots of different breads.

SPECIAL FOODS

French food is eaten all over the world. Different parts of France are famous for different sorts of food. Places near the sea are famous for fish dishes – the area around the port of Marseilles is famous for fish soup. Normandy is famous for its apple tarts.

Bakers make croissants and brioches, too. These are sweet and rich, almost like cakes.

21

MADE IN FRANCE

France sells lots of **goods** to other countries, from food and drink to cars. **Exports** have made France rich.

FACTORIES

Some factories in France make things to sell, like cars. Others process food – like turning sunflowers into sunflower oil or putting milk into bottles. Others make steel. More than half the electricity that runs factories, homes and offices is made in **nuclear power** stations.

This factory makes fuel for nuclear power stations.

CARS AND PLANES

French inventors worked on early types of cars and planes. French factories have been making cars and planes ever since. They try to use new designs and ideas (like using robots to build cars).

These Airbus planes have parts made in the UK and France.

CLOTHES

Every year there is a fashion show in Paris. People come from all over the world to look at the clothes on show.

Only Japan, the USA and Germany make more cars each year than France.

GETTING AROUND

France has very good road, rail, sea and **canal** routes for getting around. Most cities have airports, too.

RAILWAYS

France has some of the world's fastest trains, even faster than Japanese 'bullet' trains. French TGV trains can go as fast as 300 kilometres per hour.

Not all French trains are this fast. Local trains are slower.

TGV trains waiting in a Paris station. These trains run between Paris and Bordeaux.

Cities, like Paris here, have a lot of traffic and air **pollution**.

ROADS AND TUNNELS

France has a very good road system. Motorways link the major cities. You have to pay to use them. There are also lots of long straight main roads that you do not need to pay to use. They join up main towns and cities.

Road and rail tunnels link France and other countries in Europe, including Italy and the UK (by the Channel Tunnel).

RIVERS AND CANALS

Rivers and the canals that join them are used to move heavy **goods** around, especially in the north of France where there are more factories.

Paris has an underground railway, the Metro. People use it to avoid road traffic, but it gets busy, too.

25

SPORTS AND HOLIDAYS

SPORTS

Some French people like to watch and play tennis, football, golf and rugby. Some important sporting events are held in France, like the Tour de France bicycle race, the Le Mans car race, and golf and tennis matches.

The Tour de France bicycle race is held every year. People come from all over the world to watch.

Lots of French people enjoy skiing. Many children learn to ski when they are very young.

Skiing brings a lot of **tourists** to France. It is a popular sport for French people, too.

TIME OFF

People like to relax in cafés and bars, or go to the cinema or the theatre. Boules is a popular game, and is played all over France. It is like a game of marbles with balls, everyone tries to get their own ball closest to a target ball.

HOLIDAYS

Most French people take their holidays in August, when it is very hot. Many of them like to leave the towns and cities and go to the countryside or the seaside for their holidays. People with young children might visit a theme park, like Disneyland Paris or Parc Asterix, both near Paris.

Over 9 million people live in Paris. It is a big city. The Disneyland Paris theme park is one-fifth of the total size of Paris!

27

FESTIVALS AND ARTS

FESTIVALS

Some French festivals are to do with religion, but many are not. Some festivals, like Easter, are celebrated all over France. Some are local celebrations, often to do with farming or fishing.

A big French festival is Bastille Day, 14 July. It celebrates the French **Revolution** of 1789, which replaced kings with a **government** chosen by the people.

People celebrating in Nice. The festival, 'Shrove Tuesday', is just before Lent when people decide to give things up.

This picture was painted by the famous French artist Renoir in 1876.

The first French artists lived about 30,000 years ago. They painted hunters and animals on the walls of caves. The paintings are still there.

ARTS

Many famous artists, sculptors, musicians and writers have come from France. Art galleries all over the world have examples of French painting and sculpture. French artists are famous for trying out new ways of painting.

Famous artists include Claude Monet (who liked to paint landscapes) and Paul Gauguin Gauguin is famous for his brightly coloured paintings of people in Polynesia.

FRANCE FACTFILE

People

People from France are called French.

Capital city

The capital city of France is Paris.

Largest cities

Paris is the largest city in France with more than 9 million people. The second largest is Lyons. Marseilles is the third largest city.

Head of country

France is ruled by a president and a **government**.

Population

There are nearly 58 million people living in France.

Money

The money in France is called the franc.

Language

Nearly everyone speaks French. French uses the same letters as the English alphabet.

Religion

Three-quarters of French people are Roman Catholic.

GLOSSARY

canals rivers that have been made by people

exports goods sold to other countries

goods things people have made

gorge steep, narrow valley made by a river or stream

government people who run the country. In France the government is elected (chosen) by the people.

lava melted rock from a volcano

marshland low land that is wet all the time and can flood in winter

nuclear power energy that can be used as electricity

plateau a high, flat area of land

revolution when the people in a country get rid of the rulers

Roman Empire the Romans were people who, from Rome in Italy, took over much of Europe and other parts of the world from 750BC to AD 300

scrubland hot, dry places where only bushes and grass grow

tourist someone who visits a place on holiday

volcano a mountain that sometimes throws out melted rock or ash

INDEX